The Stories In Between

Teresa Forrest

Five Leaves Publications

For Rianna, Aislinn, Kealan and Steve, with love

Contents

The Stories In Between

Teresa Forrest

Published in 2023 by Five Leaves Publications
14a Long Row, Nottingham NG1 2DH
www.fiveleaves.co.uk
www.fiveleavesbookshop. co.uk

ISBN: 978-1-915434-11-1

Printed in Great Britain

Almost Home

You have grown, your years running by
on long legs, and have stamped
the soil from your half-Irish toes, dodged
the English giant who would grind
your bones into bread.
I, your mother, am formed from folklore,
spit and cabbage. When I made you,
I hadn't finished making me. I am so rough
around the edges. What worries me
is what's been left undone.
Most days I travel across the Irish Sea
on the shrill of gulls. My children – I will
spread stars out on water to light your way
home. I promise I will always be here.
Tomorrow I will translate the world
for you. But this afternoon
will be a riddle. Ask me a question.
Any question.
Yes.

Binevenagh
i.m. Ann Forrest, 1944 – 2020

Between Avish and Gortmore,
the mountain that,
with flat-plateaued fortitude
has held for 60 million years
as epochs passed…
Its shadow sweeps fields
folded into green, and towns
full of longing.

A skylark rises in song,
stills on the wind,
descends.

The mountain insists.

On fine days the sun shimmers
through clouds, consecrates
the landscape – wych elm, ash,
wild thyme, uncovering possibilities.
In those hedgerows the world turns.

Under darkening skies, I am here,
thinking of you as I turn for home.

In Ballerin Village

The fat-bellied range in my granny's house works hard,
to warm us. Get too close and it warns us with a scalding tongue.
Washing hangs limp-bodied above it. Pans hiss with home-grown
and, once, a cockerel that had crowed too early for her liking.
Always the kettles whistle to her tune.
On summer evenings I clamber weary to an attic bed.
Each morning she gives me an orange,
a small globe that feels like the world.

Passing Through

In every picture my memory took
of him, Granda wore overalls –
he who seldom spoke but would recite
the rosary every day, his fingers clasping
each bead as prayers slipped
from his lips, ascended.

Here he is rootling in the chicken coop,
his fine hands reaching to scatter
corn and poultry mash.
We watch their dipping beaks,
their scratch and bustle.

This time he stoops, as old boys do,
to cultivate his rows of praties, carrots, leeks,
this man of the soil, this earth, while I stain
my lips with stolen strawberries.

Now he shows me how to
grasp a scythe firmly, slice
through waist-high grass

he who takes his leave in the chapel plot,
soil beneath and above him.

Rooted there.

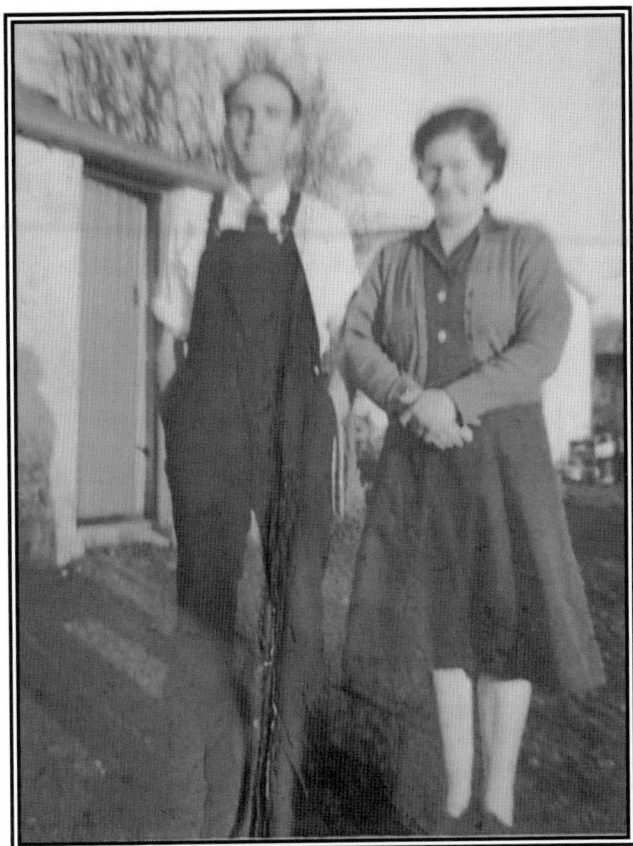

The Day My Daughter Met Finn McCool

He plays the pipes, then beckons me again
to share some tea, catch up on all the craic.
I tell my girl we'll cross the Irish Sea, then

we catch a Megabus to Scotland, and
with a hop, skip, jump, we're on the right track
while he plays the pipes and beckons us again.

His baritone grazes spires and rooftops when
he laughs. He'll tell stories from way back,
once we sail across the Irish Sea. Then

we see him through the mist, my oldest friend,
stooped a little now, carrying a stack
of memories, as he beckons us again.

When he smiles my heart hop-skips, a sudden
embrace, because he's got that stubborn knack
for sending love that crosses oceans, then

head in clouds, he narrates some long-forgotten
legends that will ignite our hearts. No lack
of love between us, watching the Irish Sea when
Finn McCool beckons us again.

Breathless Air

Limavady, 1975

The tarmac is melting in the swelter of
this August afternoon and I am barefoot,
barely six. I stretch out my toes, dab
their tips against the tacky mass.
Gangs of children slouch

on hot pavements yearning
for the thrill of raindrops on skin
or the bliss of ice cream.
Across the estate, doors gape.
There is a buzz of lawnmowers.

A bright little van putters to a stop
in the cul-de-sac, its mechanical sonata
pulling sticky-coined kids to the kerb
as teenagers flash cigarettes behind
coal sheds, listlessly kick a deflated ball

through breathless air. They stub out
conversation. Then the sky darkens
and clouds gather, restless, sullen,
until the distant brawl of thunder edges closer
and lightning snaps the sky like snipers' bullets.

Dereliction

The house was empty, a fractured carapace,
when, bold as magpies, we picked our way
past the Keep Out sign. We played
between sprawled bricks, sifted dirt
through our fingers, foraged for secrets,
raised a chipped cup high as we laughed
and grubbed for treasure, until a nail
unseen in the floorboards pierced
Dáithí's foot. His wails were a warning siren
as we hobbled him home.

By the Wayside

On my way to Canice Primary School
when I was nine or thereabouts,
I saw a boy pitched backwards
by a car. He sprawled between
kerb and road, a fledgling tipped
from the nest,

his eyes closed, head pillowed
by tarmac, face pale as eggshell,
a tuft of hair feathering out.
His legs had stopped in a cartoon run,
one shoe astray, pink heel poking

through his sock, pink belly
where his jumper had rucked up.
He just lay there, exposed to adult gaze,
unknowing as they scrambled to him,
the fingers of his right hand
curled, as if holding on.

Luvs

Carved on the desk during Mr Ludden's maths class
with a compass for which he has no other purpose,
KEVIN 4 CLIONA
It cost him
six stinging stripes per palm.

They thought that love was walking
hands on waists,
snogging by the dustbins
at the back of the school canteen,
slow-dancing at the disco
to Johnny Logan's 'What's Another Year'.

He bought her a necklace with their initials interlocked.
His eyes crinkled when he smiled at her, or smoked,
blowing rings to make her laugh,
promised he'd put a solid one on her finger
and swore that one day they'd leave this dirty old town

until Pauline Reilly with her plump pink lips
threw glances at him.
On the schoolyard wall
in permanent black marker
he scrawled
KEVIN LUVS PAULINE

Tender

Today she steps into Greta Garbo's shoes,
drags her dressing gown round her bony hips,
reaches for her Revlon as she grips
the walking frame. Some days, we can choose
to live, articulate our scripts, or lose
ourselves. Today she pops champagne and sips
then fills her glass again before she slips
some morphine in. Later, she'll refuse
to let the carers come. She turns on the Philco,
has the music hold her, still bereft,
through the final gasp of loss, an echo
of herself, now the one she loved has left.
No more flushed nights of lust or tender days,
wretched now they've gone their separate ways.

Remember That Girl From School?

You've seen her
shuffling in line at the butcher's.
Folks say she's mental, tapped, touched.
She asks for scraps, claims they're for the dog,
carts off her life
in a wheeled trolley bag.

A safety pin pinches her overcoat shut.
Buttonholes gawp. Her gloves are frayed
where pink knuckles bulge; her fingers
intertwine as if in prayer.
A murmured litany of everyday curses
reels from her lips.

She lives under stairs under
the underpass, on the outskirts of life,
this coffee cup beggar at whom
passers-by pitch copper,
this magician, who folds herself down
at night, becomes invisible. Almost.

Nightlife

A black cat sleeks, purring
like the slow hum of traffic.
Buddleia has sprawled along the front wall,
and behind its plain white door
the stone house is silent.

In the hallway, a framed photo hangs
tilted: a couple gazes into this future
where bills, letters, fliers, snag
the letterbox. Dust motes hold in moonlight.

Up in the one pale bedroom, alone,
his worn bones jolt as he
shifts to the cold side of the bed,
wraps night around himself.

And outside the black cat still sleeks.
Across town, the highway purrs with traffic.

On the Tenth Floor of the High Rise

She's painted her room the colours of the sun.
Stirring, she wakes and rubs her eyes and falls
into another day of her husband gone –
three months before now. Alone between these walls,
she curls up, cat-like, quiet in a chair
and dreams of a childhood country far away
and lost, with choro music in its air,
the flow and tilt that held her in its sway.
Choro drums a beat inside her head.
She rises, hesitant to fill the space
at first, then she begins, lightly, to thread
her way around this room, this life, with grace:
her feet begin to tap, and then her hips
start to swing, and song rolls through her lips.

Flight

I stopped her in the street to ask
how her nephew was. I'd heard
about the accident, how he'd fallen
down three flights of stairs.

Convinced that he could fly, he'd climbed
the ladder of his untethered mind,
perched on the roof, spread his arms
to roll and swoop, teetered…

She moved the conversation on,
to visiting hours, then the overcast day,
the overwhelming cost of living, how kids
are sensitive compared to us.

Perhaps he's safe with those
who'll listen to his voice, his chorus,
as morning hatches precious as an egg.

Drift

You wake, cannot find yourself,
search the bed in vain. Your silken slip,
shed like skin, has surrendered
your disguise. The mirror
returns a stranger's face. You,
who once inscribed grief on your wrists,

lean closer. The girl who loves you
is still there, not quite falling.
Later, you step out to the pavement.
People surge past,
drowning you in their wake.

Listen to the torrents
in your head. Hold fast
until small, calm waves lave you,
slow to a murmur.
Hold onto this day,
this hour, this moment,

move towards the drift and pull
of a lifetime awash
with possibility.

Closing Time, Reprise

That night you still existed:
 we walk into the arms of dusk.
A haze of rain mists pavements, clothes,
us. You slip your hand into mine

and we run, throw off damp jackets
in your yellow kitchen, slam tequila
poured from a cracked blue jug, laugh
as streetlight seeps through thin curtains.

In your room we kiss. You run your hand
over the ladder in my tights, tell me it's a stairway,
undress. Night blurs. Love
seems as certain as the moon.

Wasted

When she wakes her mouth's
a dried-up playa and her silted head
is tilting from the wildest dreams.
Her eyes open, close, flicker,
and fear scuttles through her.

Her newborn baby's keening cry,
his creamy scent. How he was taken
from her, his memory folded
into her always, innocent
as a blank page.

When morning comes, a throb of light
passes through pale curtains,
makes her retch and reach for more,
the bottle coaxing her.
She'd slip out of herself if she could,

leave her damp skin, drift off
into the night, stay there until
she is darkness.
Instead, she pours one more,
swallows it down until she is empty again.

Mrs Ritchie

She carries her anger in a handbag,
worn-out crocodile skin, used to have matching shoes.
It cost two and six from St Dymphna's thrift shop.
First port of call is Shop 'n' Save, she crams
the basket high with Barry's tea, sliced pan, Chum,
then, hurried along on the crest of a queue,
she's flotsam on the dark wet pavements,
thinks she's going under, stops off at old Joe's café,
takes the number 10 to Dedworth,
nearly home, sees Highbridge Towers pressing in,
rushes on, hears his urgent breathing,
feels his fingers on her wrist, her bag.
Young enough to be her grandson!
She claws back, knocks him down
beside the handbag, scoops up
the worn-out crocodile skin, jaws gaping.
She used to have matching shoes.

Mr Lovell

swallows his wife, bit by bit.
At breakfast, he licks the soft spoonfuls
of her blue eyes, nibbles her ears, murmurs sweet
morsels. You flash a warning glance, but her eyes
are lactescent as she pours herself out.

Greedy at lunch, he butters her up,
then sniffs her neck, sucks up her marrow,
and you tut. She seems hollow.
He goes back for seconds, helps himself
to her peachy skin, her partridge-plump cheeks.

At the dinner table he unhinges his jaw,
engulfs her head, gulps. You blubber,
cannot swallow, and stand up before
he gollops her down. Then he turns
to you and smacks his lips.

Small Worlds
after Hilda Sheehan's 'The Seal'

My loggerhead turtle never speaks.
He sits on the draining board
among soapy mugs
and looks at me through ancient eyes.

There's nowhere left for him to go.
The bath is bleached too clean.
He doesn't approve of the Toilet Duck
nestling in the loo.

He wanders into the shower,
mourns the dried up porifera,
maunders through the house, snaps
at dripping taps, at overheated rooms.

He has fallen into a reverie
of travelling back to the sea,
remembers how he once carried
small worlds on his back.

Now it's just him and me –
but I didn't ask him to come here.
He follows me like a smell,
or conscience, or regret.

At night I dream of the ocean
and we swim together
through undercurrents,
each in different worlds.

Pillow Talk

Afterwards they don't stop talking,
the sounds of their voices weaving
through the night
from that first moment
of easy laughter,
pillow talk between kisses,
how they swallow each other,
greedy as nestlings,
as night meets day's blush again
and again, carelessly wound round
one another – lips, skin, fingertips uttering

until half a smile later,
toothbrushes lean together
in a newly-fitted bathroom
and half-glances cross a breakfast table.
Time winds itself around them.
Some days spin too fast – chit chat, chit chat,
then air kisses.
Doors slam and a car bickers
into the distance each morning.
There are tiffs, squabbles, tears,
restless nights of no touching, cold pillows, harsh light

until there are no words left.

Parting

Her dressing gown: worn thin in places,
washed out, the ghost of itself
slung on a hook on the bedroom door.

She has been propped up, her face a pale moon.

His cardigan: tight-knit, neatly
patched at the elbows, cloaking the back of his chair.
He leans forward, tilts an ear towards her.

She tells him *I can't live like this*, reaches out

in a blur of movement, and white tablets,
the ones that get her through the day,
spatter the carpet like erratic thoughts.

Then silence.

Making Tracks

The train thrums, rolls out
of the station, past concrete blocks,
yards spilling debris, waste ground.

Everyone's head is in a phone,
a laptop, another world, and reflected
on a smutted windowpane.

The train thrusts on, leaving
each town, suburb, factory standing.
It slips through countryside

slices fields, blurs pine trees,
fractures sky, eases
as it nears our destination.

And in the station
a life-creased woman waits for someone
while we spill round her.

A man hesitates, lifts
his collar against the cooling air,
heads for home.

The train thrums, rolls into
the station, past cities,
towns, homes, lifetimes,
as the sun sets in a bruised sky.

Everything Must Go

When today you walk past the deadbeat
shopping centre, forgotten at the edge of town,
windows gashed like a punched mouth,
stand still in the echo of what it was and a storm
of shoppers appears like a shaken snow globe
to browse among the BOGOFs in the supermarket.
You might hear the mewl of children, scuffling past
in their knock-off Start-Rites, old enough
now to push offspring in buggies, but too young really.
Paper-skin posters peel from walls –
Closing Down Sale. All Stock Must Go! –
And weeds elbow their way through cracks where
people sat on benches to chat or smoke or sip
from Styrofoam cups or stop for just a moment.

But it's fallen by the wayside, like an old can
kicked sideways. Look at it huddled there, the worn-out
shopping centre, wearing its concrete coat.

Homecoming

Morning light, like Kenmare lace, threads
through trees as the road unspools.
Birds are stitched to telephone wires.
In a patch of green a squat farmer appears
then disappears as our lone car sweeps past.
Distant hills interrupt the skyline

and in the next village, stone cottages hewn
from landscape hold generations
beneath changing skies. Hydrangeas
cover garden walls in blue and pink blurs
while we motor onwards

to where our children will grow like wildflowers,
search for footholds among ancient grasslands.
A weave of colour, of light, for this time,
for years that unroll before us
like the road.

Five Leaves New Poetry

Five Leaves presents a new series of debut poetry pamphlets by East Midlands writers, showcasing the emerging talent from our region.

1. *She Will Allow Her Wings* **Jane Bluett**
   978-1-915434-09-8, 40 pages, £7, June 2023

2. *Beyond Caring* **Trish Kerrison**
   978-1-915434-10-4, 40 pages, £7, September 2023

3. *North by Northnorth* **Elvire Roberts**
   978-1-915434-12-8, 44 pages, £7, December 2023

4. *The Stories In Between* **Teresa Forrest**
   978-1-915434-11-1, 32 pages, £7, December 2023

5. *Keep All the Parts* **Roy Young**
   978-1-915434-13-5, 32 pages, £7, March 2024

6. *Relief Map* **Jan Norton**
   978-1-915434-14-2, 32 pages, £7, March 2024

All pamphlets can be ordered from our websites,
post-free to anywhere in the UK.

Five Leaves Bookshop/Publications
14a Long Row, Nottingham NG1 2DH
bookshop@fiveleaves.co.uk   **0115 837 3097**
www.fiveleaves.co.uk   www.fiveleavesbookshop.co.uk